The Amish

John A. Hostetler

HERALD PRESS
Scottdale, Pennsylvania
Kitchener, Ontario

Introduction

There have been many requests for a short, readable, and reliable account of Amish life. While the Amish have been mentioned from time to time in newspapers and magazines, many persons know little of their real life. The Amish themselves write very little. There has been much distortion of the subject by a few "outsiders" with good intentions but few facts.

Because Amish practices vary from place to place throughout the United States, the problem of writing a clear and complete description in a short space is very difficult. Nevertheless, the author has succeeded in presenting the biblical values and sociological principles basic to their way of life.

John A. Hostetler, the author, was born and reared in an Amish family near Belleville, Pennsylvania, in Big Valley on the Kishacoquillas. Now a sociologist and student of Pennsylvania folk culture, he holds the BS degree from Goshen College in Indiana and the MS and PhD degrees from The Pennsylvania State University.

In this booklet the reader will receive at a popular price the true story of this much-misunderstood people, the Amish.

William G. Mather, PhD
Professor of Rural Sociology
The Pennsylvania State University

Who Are the Amish?

Interest in Pennsylvania Dutch art, lore, and cookery has never been greater than in our time. Stylized designs of the tulip, fish, and *distelfink* bird decorate linens, textiles, and pottery; shoofly pie, seven sweets and seven sours appear on uncounted restaurant menus. The Amish, who want no publicity, have become the focal point of this interest, but they turn their backs to snapshot-taking tourists and ignore all of it in their quiet way.

To a surprising degree the Amish are like their fellow Americans, but in many ways they are also unlike them. Their barns and houses, their lullabies and proverbs, are similar to other Pennsylvania-Dutch-speaking groups, but different from the rest of America. There are many religious groups among the Pennsylvania-Dutch-speaking Americans. Those groups who have captured the public attention by their otherworldly dress are called "plain people." Pennsylvania Dutch people who do not dress "plain" are known as the "fancy" Dutch. The Amish are the plainest of the plain people, but they are not the only plain-garbed people.

The Amish are gentle and industrious farmers. As a late seventeenth-century offshoot of the Mennonites, they took their name from Jacob Amman of Switzerland, who stood for the epitome of conservatism.

Three great values are cherished by the Amish people: a devout religion, an agrarian way of life, and a cohesive family and community.

The highest value and ultimate goal for the Amish is eternal life. Like evangelical Protestants, the Amish believe in the supremacy of the Bible. But unlike most Protestants, the Amish believe they must be separate from the world in order to attain eternal life.

A visit to the Pennsylvania State Museum

Like Luther and other Reformers, they believed that religion was an individual matter and that no church could dispense divine grace through its organization or hierarchy.

The Amish founders felt that the great Reformers did not go far enough in reforming the medieval church. From a renewed study of the Bible they said that infant baptism was not valid, but that a person should be baptized after confessing his faith; that the church and state should be separate, and they wanted absolute freedom in religious affairs. The believer, they said, must not bear arms, nor swear oaths, but follow the peaceful example of Christ in all things regardless of the consequences.

The consequences were suffering and death. They suffered as heretics by the hand of church and state alike, being burned at the stake and tied to wagon wheels. Many were placed in sacks and thrown into the river, and they were tortured in other cruel ways. Those who survived fled to the hills of Switzerland, Germany, and Alsace. Many came to America when William Penn extended his general invitation to persecuted people in Europe.

The Amish regard very highly the customs and beliefs of their forefathers. This explains why they have clung to the manner of worship, styles of dress, and traditions of centuries past. Did their forefathers have automobiles, tractors, telephones, electric lights, church buildings? No! And with few exceptions the Old Order Amish continue to plow with horses, travel in buggies, and assemble in homes for worship.

While both Mennonites and Amish came from the same seventeenth-century background, today they differ in many ways. Except for a very small group called Old Order Mennonites, the Mennonites have not held so closely to traditions. Mennonites worship in church buildings, maintain their own colleges, conduct missionary activity, publish literature, and administer worldwide relief service, none of which the Amish do as a corporate group. The Old Order Amish do not attempt to convert outsiders nor do they hold "revival" meetings.

According to them the greatest wisdom is to despise the

A Midwestern buggy with reflective tape and license plate for non-motor vehicle. Old surrey carriages from the last century are remade into Amish styles. This is a family "rig" with solid rubber tire rims, taboo in many communities.

"world" and to love God. To seek wealth and to rely upon it is worldly. When oil was discovered on Amish farms in Kansas a few years ago, they sold their farms and moved out of the state. To pursue honors or high dignity and to "raise oneself" through fashionable dress, education, office-holding, or any other way is worldly. To provide adequate sustenance for the family is necessary,

7

but luxuries and superfluities and lustful appetites the Amishman regards as harmful to the soul. The Amishman would agree with the fourteenth-century monk Thomas a Kempis that a poor peasant who serves God is better than a proud philosopher.

In Twenty States

Amish colonists first settled in Berks, Chester, and Lancaster counties in southeastern Pennsylvania. The first ship to carry persons with typical Amish names was *The Adventure*, which sailed from Rotterdam and arrived in Philadelphia on October 2, 1727, but it is almost certain that a few families arrived before this time.

In their search for fertile farm lands they migrated to many states, so that today Amish communities may be found in twenty states and in Ontario. Over 80 percent of the members are in Ohio, Indiana, and Pennsylvania. Common family names are Bontrager and Miller in Indiana, Yoder and Miller in Ohio, and Beiler and Stoltzfus in Pennsylvania.

The Amish do not live in cloistered villages. They live as families in the countryside and around small rural towns. Their farms are interspersed among "English" (non-Amish) farm homes. The Amish are not a commune but a religious community constituting a subculture in America. There are over a hundred settlements or regions where the Amish live. Each settlement is divided into "church districts" (congregations). The number of households in each district varies but they seldom exceed forty families. The districts are deliberately kept small so that their gatherings for worship can be accommodated in a farm home or barn. The total Amish population (with children) numbered about 90,000 in 1982.

Because of their high birth rate the Amish have been one of the fastest-growing religious groups in America. Even though they lose some of their children to more progressive churches, their rate of growth is still increasing. And this has been happening in spite of the

Sunday dress of teenage girls

Photo by Melvin J. Horst

prediction of some that they are doomed to extinction in the modern world.

The Amish have completely disappeared from their European homeland and there are no Amish churches on the continent. Those who remained in Europe have been absorbed into other churches. That they have survived in America, supposedly the "melting pot" of the world, has captured the interest of social scientists.

Preaching Services

Families living within a limited geographical area, called a "district," take turns having preaching services in their home. In summer, services are frequently held on the *Dreshden* (threshing) floor of the barn. Each Amish *Gemeinde* (congregation) contains from fifteen to thirty families or about seventy-five baptized members. There is generally one bishop for each district with two or three assisting preachers and a deacon. When there are too many people in one district, it is divided and a new set of preachers is ordained for the new district.

To get ready for preaching services a family must work hard and cooperate in many ways. Stables must be cleaned and yards put in order; furniture must be moved, and frequently heating stoves are

Backless church benches are transported from house to house and used every two weeks for the three-hour-long preaching service.

Photo by Charles S. Rice

polished, walls painted, and fences whitewashed. The meeting benches must be hauled and put in proper place, which often means removing the panel walls and doors between first-floor rooms. On Saturday before preaching a dozen or more women arrive to bake bread and pies and see that the supply of pickles, red beets, jams, and coffee is adequate for the meal which will be served after the worship service.

Only sick persons may stay home from preaching services. Even the six-week-old baby must attend. As they gather for the sacred occasion, everyone exchanges a handshake. Preachers greet each other with the holy kiss as commanded in the Bible (1 Thessalonians 5:26). The meeting begins about 9:00 a.m. or earlier and frequently lasts until 1:00 p.m. They sing the slow tunes of the *Ausbund* hymnal in unison, two sermons are preached, silent and oral prayers read, and short testimonies (*Zeugniss*) are offered by all the Amish preachers present.

Amish children learn to sit through all this, although their preoccupation with handkerchiefs (making such objects as "mice" or a "cradle and baby") helps to pass the time. Cookies or "half-moon pies" (in Pennsylvania) served to toddlers during mid-service help to reduce their restlessness. Not only children, but frequently some adults fall asleep during the long, chanted sermons.

Lunch and the social hour following the services are considered a valuable part of the meeting. The after-church menu is standard and so fixed by custom. Everyone enjoys the period of visiting and good fellowship which follows. Not only do they discuss religious subjects, but also the happenings of the day, crops and farming, world events, and their own community problems.

Preaching is held once every two weeks. On alternate Sundays the family dresses up and stays at home to rest, but not by a radio or television set! They may also visit uncles, aunts, or cousins. They learn to know their families well by playing, reading, resting, hiking, or doing things together.

Amish bishops, preachers, and deacons are chosen from their own lay members by "lot" for life, and there is no place for specialized training. They receive no salary. There is no need for constructing a costly church building when services are held in homes. Amish bishops are the ones who administer the discipline, but major decisions must be endorsed by "the voice" (vote) of each member.

Family and Community

The Amish family is a strong social unit, notable for its stability and the contentment of its members. Children are wanted. Homes are effective teaching agencies. The meaning of hard work and cooperation is learned early in life.

The task of homemaking has not been lightened by electrical appliances, although many homes do have modern plumbing. The Amish mother never considers working outside the home and at the same time trying to raise a family. There is plenty of time to bear children, and to "bring them up in the nurture and admonition of

Typical Amish costume. The young man is wearing a telescopic hat.

the Lord." The size of the completed family is on the average between six and seven children. Divorce is not permitted and desertion or separation is rare.

Grandfather is respected as a patriarch, and his social status increases as he reaches retirement age. He would be insulted by old-age pension checks. To retire he simply moves into the *grossdawdy* (grandfather) house, and the younger generation takes over. He shuns commercial forms of insurance, for in his judgment he already has the best kind of insurance. He has no premiums to pay. If a barn burns down, the neighbors are there to help him build a new one. If he becomes ill, they do his work. Should he die suddenly, they make arrangements to have the farm operations continue.

Amish mutual aid provides "social security" for its members from birth to death. Security comes from friendly personal relations, from father and mother, brother and sister, uncle and aunt, and church members, and not from impersonal and remote sources, such as investment bonds, state security, or welfare boards.

For the past number of years Amish leaders have appeared in Washington to seek freedom from federal aid. They do not object to

Funeral procession, on the way to a plain Amish cemetery in the open country.

Photo by Melvin J. Horst

Photo by Charles S. Rice

Mutual aid, once widespread among rural people, is still practiced by the Amish. Many are skillful carpenters.

paying taxes, but they do object to receiving government aid or having their children and grandchildren fall heir to such a temptation. Before the House Ways and Means Committee they said, "Old-age survivors insurance is abridging and infringing to our religious freedom. Our faith has always been sufficient to meet the needs as they come." They believe, as the Bible says, "But if any provide not . . . for those of his own house, he hath denied the faith, and is worse than an infidel" (1 Timothy 5:8).

Compulsory welfare systems, the consolidation of small rural schools, and conscription have been the major threats to the Amish community. Their attitude toward the government is essentially like their forefathers. They acknowledge the necessity of government and its right to keep order. Some Amish will vote on election day but they will not run for public office. That would place an Amish person in a position of having to exercise "worldly" power which is forbidden by his religion. The Amish are forbidden to take an oath, and they will not use courts to settle disputes among themselves. In addition to supporting their schools and caring for their aged, they pay all taxes required of United States citizens.

The Amishman who lives by his standards enjoys a secure and self-sufficient family and community life. However rigid others may think his religion and culture are, it is a mistake to assume that he is a slave to an unhappy life. Children born into his home are loved and wanted, eat well, and are clothed and housed adequately. He has no fear of losing his job, nor does he wonder where the bread will come from for his wife and children.

Amish Economy

There is a popular notion that an Amishman has plenty of good hard cash, and that he can dig it out of his pants pocket on demand. The idea has no foundation, but is easy to believe since the Amishman often pays his bills in cash.

The stability of the Amish agricultural community has few equals in the nation. A spokesman for the National Catholic Rural Life Conference called the Amish "the finest rural culture which we have been able to observe. . . ." Although the Old Order Amish still use horse-drawn farm implements, their farms are known for their fertility and productiveness.

They know how to transform poor land into productive farms. The Amish formula is simply rotation of corn, small grain, legumes, and a cash crop, with plenty of barnyard manure, lime, and fertilizer. This is combined with hard work and, generally, careful management.

Profits are put back into the soil. As a whole the Amish income is probably less than that of the average farmer. He does not have the expense of maintaining automobiles and high-cost machinery, but his gross income is somewhat limited. He is not a "money grabber," but he firmly believes in saving. The Amishman is not a large-scale owner or operator. He wants no more land than necessary to raise a family.

The Amish raise corn, oats, and a variety of hay crops for their animals, and they grow many vegetables for family use. An Amish farm generally has horses, dairy cattle, hogs, poultry, and often sheep. The Amish people are very selective in adopting modern inventions, especially avoiding those which would erode their togetherness as a community and family.

Religion has set certain limits to agricultural practices as it has in social life. Special agricultural benefits from the government are refused. No truck may enter an Amish farm on Sunday to pick up produce or milk; many families churn their weekend milk into butter. Some communities, either because of Sunday complications or because of objections to modernizing their cow barn, have established cheese factories to process whole milk. Should the Amish adopt the latest invention, the milk storage tank, milk would then

Aspirations for horsemanship and farming start early in life.

Photo by Melvin J. Horst

not need to be picked up every day. On the other hand, dairying may become so competitive and highly organized that it will become impossible to do it any way but the "worldly" way.

Language

All Amish in the United States speak the Pennsylvania "Dutch" (German) language. Some of the Alsatian Amish spoke French when they came to America in the last century and Swiss is still spoken among some Indiana Amish. Contrary to popular opinion, the Amish are not the only Pennsylvania-Dutch-speaking people in America. Others who speak it include Lutherans, Reformed, persons of Evangelical United Brethren background, Church of the Brethren (Dunkards), Brethren in Christ, and some Mennonites.

Anyone becoming acquainted with the Amish will discover that they use three languages: Pennsylvania Dutch, High German, and English. The Pennsylvania Dutch dialect is not a degenerate form of German but a dialect of high German resembling that still spoken in the Palatine or Rhineland area of modern Germany. The Amish speak this dialect in their homes, but they have not reduced it to writing. When the child is old enough for school, he must learn to speak English.

The English language is used when the Amishman goes into the "English" community, that is, when he goes to town or talks to an "English" (non-Dutch-speaking) person. A guest at an Amish table should not be surprised if dialect chatter prevails at one end of the table while family members seated near him keep the conversation in English.

Their third language is High German. Its use is associated with functions of worship: for Bible reading (in Luther's translation), preaching, praying, and singing hymns. Although parents teach their children a reading knowledge of the Bible, most Amish know High German only passively and can scarcely carry on a conversation in it.

English spoken in a Dutch manner frequently seems hind-fore-

Photo by Charles S. Rice

Lancaster County, Pennsylvania, farm. Large double house serves the farm family as well as the grandparents. Summer kitchens are common among the Amish.

most to the visitor. But the people who make Dutch wares and decorate them with proverbs and wise sayings have mixed up the "Dutch" far out of proportion to its natural usage.

If an Amishman looks at his hair in the mirror as he gets out of bed, he looks *stroovlich*. When memory does not function properly or is slightly mixed up, he may say he is *ferhoodlt*. The seamstress uses the same word when her thread gets all tangled up. When a youngster does not sit still, the Amishman tells the child to stop *rootching*. When he feels a few raindrops on his brow, it is *spritzing* and "it is making down."

Folk Art and Beauty

Pride manifested by individuals is regarded as a sin. Thus fashionable dress and display of wealth and luxury are taboo. But the

19

Amish have never deprived themselves of color in the sense of some colonial iconoclasts. When shared by the group, certain highly colored, useful things made by their own hands are permissible. Amish-made chairs and tables painted in traditional Pennsylvania Dutch style are widely sought. Amish quilts and hooked and braided rugs are original in design and exquisitely made. Amish gardens can be spotted for their flourishing variety of flowers.

While women's dresses must be of solid color, many are intense maroon, purple, pink, orange, or blue. China closets filled with colorful dishes, and large picture calendars, things which combine utility with beauty, are a particular delight.

One can find in Amish homes such motifs as the dove, rose, heart, tree of life, and peacock on "show" towels, illuminated hand drawings, cards of friendship, family registers, and needlecraft. But not much *Fraktur*, or illuminated handwriting, is presently being done by Amish hands.

The Amish do not paint geometric designs or "hex" signs on their barns. It is the "fancy" Dutch who use hex signs, but not as legend would have it, to keep witches away.

Courting

Amish dating is called "running around." When a boy (or girl) is old enough, usually sixteen, he attends the Sunday evening "singings" and this soon makes him eligible for dating. After three or more dates a young man may ask his girl, "Do you want to go for steady, or for so?"

Boys often have their first date arranged for them after a singing. This is known as "getting propped up." A young man going steady will tell his bashful friend, "Let me prop it up for you." He arranges for the date and thus saves the beginner some embarrassment.

After chores are done on Sunday evening the young folks prepare for the singing. The young man dresses in his best, brushes his hat and suit, and makes sure that his horse and "rig" are neat and clean. He may take his sister to the singing, or if he takes his girl he

It all began in 1942 . . .

Jacob Zook "The Hex Man" finishing a large "rain" sign soon to be placed on a Pennsylvania barn with its promise for rain during a recent dry spell.

ABOUT THE HEX SIGN YOU BUY...

Jacob Zook is a hexologist and his designs have traveled to the 50 states, to Presidents, and a King. They are sold around the world.

He did the "Irish Hex" sign for President Kennedy. This design dates back to that cold winter when General Washington's armies were camped at Valley Forge.

In 1979, struck by an incredible wave of injuries, the Phillies turned to him for help and had him place his "good luck" sign over their dug out.

He did an 8 foot "fertility" hex for Longwood Gardens.

The "Mighty Oak" sign which means "strength in Character, Body and Mind" was used by the United States Navy for one of their fighter planes.

In 1983 he wrote and published an encyclopedia of Lancaster County, the book, "The Most Asked Questions about the Pennsylvania Dutch Country and the Amish." An earlier book, "HEXOLOGY The History and meaning of the Hex Symbols" published in 1962 has gone thru it's 16th printing, and is an all time best seller.

For those who appreciate True Craftsmanship, Jacob Zook offers a Collection of 28 Originally Designed Hex Signs.

→ IF IT DOESN'T SAY Zook
IT'S NOT ORIGINAL! ←

1 DOUBLE DISTELFINK
for double good luck

2 MIGHTY OAK
for strength

4 UNICORNS
virtue and piety

5 IRISH HEX
Dutch-Irish good luck

6 SUN, RAIN & FERTILITY
abundance in fields, barn & home

7 LOVE & ROMANCE
for bliss & happiness

8 VILKUM SIGN
home "welcome" sign

10 "8" POINTED STAR
abundance & good will

11 SINGLE DISTELFINK
good luck & happiness

12 DADDY HEX
grandaddy of all hexes

15 AMISH CARRIAGE HORSE
protects barn & livestock

16 HERFORD
protects barn & livestock

17 MARRIAGE SIGN
to insure a long blissful marriage

18 "12" PETAL ROSETTE
each month a joyous one

19 COLONIAL EAGLE
a symbol of strength renewal & independence

22 DOUBLE HEADED EAGLE
strength & courage

23 HAUSE-SAGEN
house blessing

27 MAPLE LEAF
appreciation of life's beauty

28 LOVE & PEACE

30 NEW VILKUM SIGN
home "welcome" sign

31 GOOD LUCK, LOVE & HAPPINESS

32 HAPPY HEART

33 LOVE & FRIENDSHIP

34 BLESS THIS CHILD

35 HOSPITALITY

© 1983 - Jacob Zook, Paradise, Pa.

Sitting room: Amish-made carpets, rugs, wall hooks instead of clothes closets, and panel doors that are removed for preaching services. The cutaway coat is a *Mutze*, the Sunday coat of all male members.

will arrange to pick her up about dusk, perhaps at her home or at the end of a lane or at a crossroad. In some localities the young folks meet in crossroad villages to pair off in couples. Considerable secrecy pervades the entire period of courtship.

Other occasions when young folks get together are husking bees, weddings, apple *schnitzins* (apple-peeling and cutting parties), and frolics. In addition to taking his girl home after the singing, the boy who has a steady girl will see her every week or two on Saturday nights. Before entering the home of his girl he makes sure that the old folks are in bed. When his flashlight focuses on her window, the girl knows that her suitor has arrived. They spend several hours together in the "sitting room," and they do not usually leave the home on such occasions.

Bundling has for a long time been associated with Amish courtship. According to the dictionary, bundling is a practice where lovers sleep or lie together on the same bed without undressing. It is a very old custom, stemming from Oriental as well as European and New England sources, and since the Old Order Amish have retained a whole way of life characteristic of two or three centuries ago, it is only natural that they should have retained bundling. Amish leaders have tried to stamp out bundling for over a century and they have now largely succeeded. It has been a source of "church trouble" and of migrations from certain communities in the past. Sexual transgressions are strongly condemned among the Amish and the

A spirited horse and an open buggy, the prized possessions of a young man of courting age.

rate of illegitimacy is very low. Teenage youngsters in our American society are undoubtedly exposed to more tragedy and temptation than are Amish youth.

In a few instances educated people and medical authorities have been shocked by the lack of biological knowledge among the Amish. The presence of extreme guilt complexes among them has been reported by some. This is usually attributed to their indifference to higher education. Rumors of "drinking parties," of Amish boys owning automobiles secretively, and of girls wearing "English" clothing when they work as maids in town occasionally reach the outside world. It is unfair to generalize how widespread such practices are since each community has its own peculiarities.

The blue-gate story, that an Amishman paints his gate blue to announce that he has a marriageable daughter, is a myth. Robin-blue is a recurring color, but there is no connection between the daughter and the front gate or blue paint. But the legend will probably outlive the Amish.

Weddings

November brings excitement and good times to Amish communities, for it brings the wedding season. Weddings are the most important social events of the year. They are attended by as many as four hundred guests.

When a young man wants to get married, he informs the deacon or a minister of his choice, who obtains the consent of the girl's parents. Of course, the parents have known the intentions of the couple and have even made secretive plans for the wedding. After everything is formally cleared, the banns are published in church one or two Sundays prior to the date set for the wedding, which is by tradition on a Tuesday or Thursday. Early Monday morning the *Hochzeiter* (groom) sets out to contact personally all the people who are invited to the wedding, some for the whole day and others, more distant relatives and neighbors, for the evening.

In Amish life there is nothing comparable to engagement.

The bride and groom and their attendants *(naave hocker)* seated at the *Eck.*

There are no formal announcements other than the oral announcement in church. Engagement or wedding rings are not used.

The bride and groom wear new clothes, but they are made over the same pattern as their usual Sunday clothes. Blue is a favorite color of the bride. To get married it is necessary to hold a church service, starting in the morning and ending at noon. This is followed by festivities at the bride's home, where all guests are seated at tables for the noon and evening feasts. The bride and groom are seated at the *Eck* or bridal corner, which is loaded with special cakes and goodies. They are attended by two unwed couples. When evening comes, all young people, including bashful boys, must sit by a partner at the table. Following the meals the guests sing and visit for hours.

A Lancaster County, Pennsylvania, custom requires that the groom be tossed over the fence by the single men and that the bride step over a broom. They are then prepared for their new domestic role. The couple spends their wedding night in the bride's home, and they help with the clean-up work the following day. They may then spend several weeks visiting the uncles and aunts. This is the only honeymoon they will have.

Leisure

Weddings provide opportunity for "barn" games in the few places where they are not forbidden. The barn floor is swept and cleaned. Lanterns are hung from the crossbeams of the *overden* (haymow). These folk games involve a good deal of holding hands and swinging partners. Some of the common ones are *O-Hi-O, Skip to My Lou, The Needle's Eye,* and *Six Steps Forward—I Do, I Do.* Other forms of dancing and theater-going are strictly taboo among the Amish.

While weddings seem to be the high point of relaxation and enjoyment, there are many occasions when visiting is the favorite pastime. Every other Sunday is open for visiting, as worship is held bimonthly. Special days are observed by visiting, such as New Year's Day, Epiphany (Old Christmas), Easter Sunday, Ascension Day, Pentecost Monday, Thanksgiving, and Christmas. In some places Easter Monday and the day following Christmas are also observed, a survival of European custom.

Mosch Balle (literally "mush ball," but usually translated "Corner Ball") is a favorite game played among Pennsylvania Amish at sales and on other weekday occasions where young men gather together. The ball is thrown between men standing at four corners and after the ball is "hot" it is peppered at the person standing inside the square. Tug of war, racing, jumping rope, and high jumping are played by schoolchildren.

Among older children *botching* is a popular game. Two persons seated on chairs clap hands and knees alternately in various ways and quite rapidly. The feet may be used to keep time to the tune of *Darling Nelly Gray* or *Pop Goes the Weasel.*

Cigar smoking is a pastime indulged in by adult Amish men in some localities. In Lancaster County, Pennsylvania, tobacco is one of the main cash crops grown by the Amish. In other locations the use of tobacco is discouraged or even forbidden. The use of alcoholic beverages is officially discouraged. The Amish believe that since God made the animals it is proper to go to the zoo or to see a circus parade where animals are exhibited.

Medieval Music

The oldest Protestant hymnbook in the world is the *Ausbund,* the hymnal still used by the Amish. It contains words but no music. The first-known edition appeared in Switzerland in 1564, and over thirty printings have since appeared. Many of the hymns were written by Mennonite martyr forefathers who were imprisoned at Passau, Bavaria, while awaiting death sentences. They express a deep sense of humility and an overwhelming dependence upon Christ. One finds wails of loneliness, sorrow, and protest against the world of wickedness, but there is also a prominent note of triumph, and prayer for endurance in suffering.

The triumphant testimony of these martyrs who died four centuries ago is vivid to the Amishman. The martyr book *(Martyrs Mirror)* and the hymnal, along with a few present-day unhappy experiences with local draft boards and school boards, have nurtured in many of the Amish the belief that they have been and are a persecuted people.

Their tunes have been handed down for hundreds of years entirely from memory. Their singing, which is always in unison, sounds almost like a chant, with many slurs and variations. Indeed, "slow tunes" sound like medieval droning or wailing, rather than singing, to the outsider. It sometimes takes a minute to sing a single line of a verse, or twenty or thirty minutes for one hymn. The *Vorsanger* (song leader) sings in solo the first syllable of every line, then all join in.

At weddings and young people's gatherings the *Lieder Samm-lungen* or small hymnal is used. Songs in this volume are sung to so-called "fast tunes," borrowed from American Gospel songs. Though the words are German, the tunes used include "Silent Night," "Beulah Land," "Sweet Hour of Prayer," and others.

26

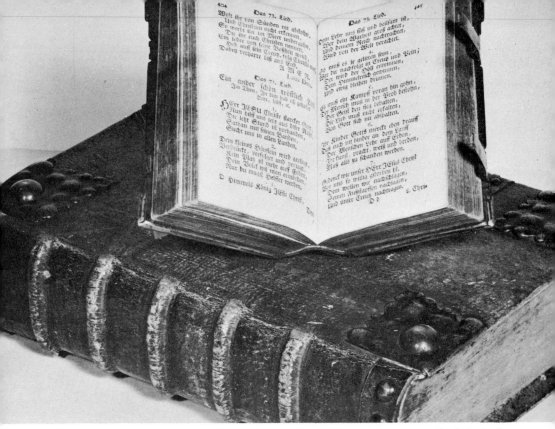

Old books for a steadfast faith. The large *Martyrs Mirror*, produced in the Netherlands and later at Ephrata, and the *Ausbund* (with buckles) are two favorite books in Amish homes.

"God has given us voices to sing his praise; then why should we use musical instruments?" said one Amishman.

Bonnets and Broadbrims

The Amish have retained dress styles which were common in their part of Europe during the seventeenth and eighteenth centuries. There has been gradual change among them, so that dress varies in regions, but they have not adopted the styles and fashions of the American society.

27

The beard is required of all adult male members of the church, and it must begin to appear at the time of baptism or marriage, depending on the local practice. Mustaches are taboo. Buttons are used on men's shirts, trousers, and underwear, and on children's dresses, but hooks and eyes are required on men's coats and vests, especially on Sunday clothing. Men's trousers are the old broad-fall type, also called "barn-door britches" (like sailor pants), and they are homemade, as are most Amish garments.

Peculiar to men's dress (for adult members of the church) is the *Mutze*, a special kind of coat with a split tail which must always be worn for church. This was the name for the ordinary coat worn by all men in the Palatinate region where the Amish lived. It was originally made of undyed flax, therefore light in color rather than dark as now.

Women wear a head covering, tied at the neck, which they call a *Kapp* (cap). All women, even very little girls, wear a white cap— except that teenage girls until marriage wear a black cap with a white organdy apron for full Sunday dress. Baby boys wear dresses and little bonnets but no *Kapp*.

Mennonites and some of the more progressive Amish groups justify the wearing of the white cap with a passage from the Bible, but with the Old Order Amish it is simply a part of the daily dress and custom. The Amish *Kapp* is an exact replica of the headpiece worn generally by Palatine women long ago.

Another part of woman's dress, originally functional but now ornamental, is the *Lepple* (bustle), a rounded piece of cloth attached at the waist on the back of the dress. It is found in eastern United States and among the "Swiss" Amish in Indiana. Its origin is also European. To many of the Amish women today it is a symbol of humility.

Women wear black bonnets over their *Kapp* as extra protection in winter. Bonnets were earlier worn by the fashionable people of France and England. The Quakers adopted them later. With a small

Women's Sunday dress with bonnets, shawls, white cap, apron, and kerchief or *halsduch*.

group of extremely conservative Pennsylvania Amish the bonnet is still taboo. They wear a kerchief and a flat hat which was probably the standard practice of all colonial Amish women settlers in this country.

Amish hats for men are made of imported Australian rabbit fur and are manufactured by special firms. One firm makes twenty-eight different sizes and nearly as many styles. The brims and crowns range in size and shape to fit a two-year-old boy or his grandfather and all ages in between. The bishop sometimes wears a special hat with a rounded crown and different curl of the brim. Adult young men may have a "telescopic" hat.

Horse and Buggy Travel

A stranger driving through an Amish community must make allowance for Amish buggies. Buggies on highways are dangerous. The threat of sudden death on the highway does not seem to bother the Amishman. Some states have recently constructed berms along the highway for buggies, thus making travel safer for all. Indiana has recently passed a law that all buggies on the highway must be licensed.

Why do the Amish use buggies instead of cars? This was the mode of travel years ago, and the Amish have retained it, like many other things, on the principle that "the old is the best." To accept the automobile would lead to a breakdown of their community life and would open the floodgates of social and cultural change. The limitations of the horse and buggy keep the social life of the family in bounds. Life is spent largely in the family and community, rather than outside of it. An Amish person has a deep sense of loyalty to his church.

Amish will ride in trains, buses, and automobiles, but to own or operate automobiles is a different matter. Many of them travel widely throughout the United States to visit relatives or see the landscape.

Every sizable community has a buggy and harness shop. One firm in Indiana makes as many as 800 buggies a year. The details of buggy design vary from Iowa to Pennsylvania. A two-seated top buggy is strictly for the family, while a one-seated topless buggy is preferred by the young man of courtship age. Some of the young men of courting age have added sporting features to their buggies, including signal lights, dimmer switch, compass, and hat rack.

Farm and Kitchen

Parents want their children to acquire the basic skills of reading, writing, and arithmetic. Their children usually attend the public elementary schools, and Amishmen have sometimes served on school boards. But they contend that after completing the elementary grades their youth should get further practical learning in farming and home management at home rather than theoretical learning in the schools. In speaking of higher education, one Amishman said, "Education is all right for some people but not for our kind of people." Another said, "Education does not build muscle like tilling the soil in the open field and sunshine."

Horse-drawn carriages and high-speed vehicles sometimes clash. Here a frightened horse jumped into the path of an oncoming trailer truck.

Photo by Indiana State Police

The Amish draw a sharp line between the kind of education their youth get in the elementary school and that which they would receive in high school. Amish fathers have gone to jail rather than subject their children to the secular influences of the modern high school. They have generally opposed school consolidation, for not only would their children feel strange in a large school where competitive athletic sports, gym classes, and activities not directly related to farming are required but they would be unnecessarily exposed to temptation.

Amish parents are undoubtedly right in sensing the potential danger of the modern high school to their community life. Should their children attend the local public high school, they would probably no longer want to be either farmers or Amish. Sociologists have pointed out that the high school, even in a rural setting, is essentially a leveler of rural and urban culture. The Amish people want at all costs to conserve an agricultural way of life with its traditional values.

Today all Amish communities maintain private country schools, taught by their own noncollege-trained teachers. The schools are closely integrated with family life, with farm and rural enterprises, and with their religious beliefs. The U.S. Supreme Court (Wisconsin v. Yoder, 1972) upheld the right of the Amish to maintain their school practices. On completion of the elementary grades, the states are restrained from compelling the Amish to attend high school. The Amish feel morally responsible to raise their children to thrive on cooperation and humility and to limit the exposure of their children to those middle-class values which would erode their community life.

Normally the Amish child begins to assist his parents when be is four or five years old, and he is given some responsibility at the age of five or six. Boys are introduced to farming operations, and they almost invariably develop a keen interest in farming. Girls are taught to perform small tasks for their mothers and learn the arts of cooking and housekeeping. Nothing pleases Amish parents quite so much as to have their children grow up be honest, industrious, and thrifty adults.

Yoder School, a public school, near Grantsville, Maryland, where Amish state-school relations are at their best.

Disciplining the child often becomes necessary, and this is usually done by *bletching* (spanking). The instrument used may be the palm of the hand or a fresh switch from a tree. The Amish agree with Solomon: "He that spareth his rod hateth his son." Their formula for delinquency is stern discipline and generous family security.

Stress and Change

Many pressures are exerted on the Amish way of life. Although change is slow, it is inevitable. Some of their members leave the Old Order and join a more "progressive" church. When a boy leaves, the typical expression is, "He got his hair cut," or if he goes completely outside the Amish and Mennonite world, then, "He went English." A few girls go all the way to the world of lipstick, permanents, high heels, and the ways of the charm school.

33

Mental illness is probably as prevalent among the Amish as it is in modern society. They have their proportion of suicides too. Those who leave the culture frequently find that it takes a long time to adjust to the larger society.

Thieves have paid visits to the Amish and gangs have done their share of devilment. Stones and bricks have been thrown through Amish windows, and the law has even caught up with a few persons who admitted setting fire to Amish barns. Amish children frequently are greeted with jeers and stones by other children when they migrate into new regions. All this leaves deep marks on personality and is a most subtle pressure on the Amish to conform to the larger society.

New inventions and technology have a significant influence on the Amish community. Generally, change is accepted in small amounts. The tendency toward unlimited growth as taken for granted in modern society, and the trend to be ruled by "worldly" efficiency and convenience, is resisted. Instead, the Amish people try to adopt machines which are suited to their scale. There are some Amish, however, called "New" Amish and others called "Beachy" Amish, who permit tractors for farming and who have electricity and

Spike-tooth harrowing with single-line leader. A tug on the line and "Gee" or "Haw" give directions for turning.

Photo by Charles S. Rice

telephones in their homes. Many who cannot afford the high cost of land in their home communities will start new settlements in other areas. Some will work in small industries or in Amish-owned repair shops, or in construction work.

The Amish find no biblical grounds for opposing modern health practices. Like any of us who need an operation or emergency care, they want the best. But like many rural people, they still consult the almanac and believe in home remedies and in "rubdowns" as forms of cure.

Amish Knowledge

The Amish are not ignorant of world events. Their conversation with the visitor and salesman is often about happenings in Washington, Europe, or about an airplane crash in some remote corner of the earth. They have a sprightly humor too, and Amish hospitality is unsurpassable!

Some Amish vote. Except where there is a religious tenet at stake, they avoid going to court. Some are eloquent speakers, and for some, self-education has achieved remarkable results. Many subscribe to a local daily newspaper; many also read farm magazines and religious publications.

The weekly newspaper most widely read is *The Budget*, published at Sugarcreek, Ohio, by a non-Amish small town editor. His "national edition" (without a bit of national news) circulates in more than thirty states. Amish from most Amish communities contribute detailed accounts of news and happenings for other Amish readers. Persons who take an extended journey write what they have seen, where they slept, where they took meals, and bits of humor about their journey. The Amish have a great concern for health and in these newsletters they mention who is ill, who was born or died, who fell down the cellar steps, or who was kicked by a horse. A few major problems, such as scarcity of land, are mentioned. Throughout the year this paper keeps family and community ties strong by the reporting of ordinary events as well as special happenings.

There have been several books written by Amishmen. These are usually written by fathers for their children, and most frequently published after the death of the writer. Jonathan Fisher, a notable Amish traveler, circled the globe and wrote a book concerning his observations.

Near the close of his life, one of their most widely known bishops, Eli J. Bontreger, noted that he had traveled on all but two of the major railways of the United States and Canada. He had traveled a total of over 466,000 miles by rail and over 60,000 miles by bus and by automobile.

Hope for the Future

What contribution have the Amish made to society? What do the Amish hope to accomplish?

Although much in a Broadway musical, *Plain and Fancy*, is not true to life, Papa Yoder in speaking to the city man expresses Amish ideals superbly: "We know who we are, Mister. Don't interfere.... Look around you, Mister! Look in your world, and look here! Poor people you have plenty, and worried people and afraid. Here we are not afraid. We do not have all your books and learning, but we know what is right. We do not destroy; we build only.... And wars we don't arrange." (Used by permission of the authors and publishers. © 1954 by Chappell & Co., N.Y.)

Amish faith forbids participation in war, but they are sensitive to the sufferings of other people and they are generous contributors to foreign relief, a fact not too well known. In postwar years they gave thousands of dollars for refugee rehabilitation and foreign relief through the Mennonite Central Committee, which coordinates the relief activities of the Mennonites. Many communities have canned meat and fruits for foreign shipment.

The Amish have a strong attachment to the soil and to the Bible. Their generous brotherhoods, numbering over fifty settlements in this land, are made up of hard-working and generally prosperous people. Their neighborliness, self-control, good will, and thrift contribute immeasurably to the foundations of our civilization. They

36

have no ambitions to possess the whole world or to convert it. There will always be politicians, policemen, and military personnel, and enough people to perform these functions, they contend; but candidates for the biblical way of life which nonresistant Christians alone can fulfill are altogether too few.

Will the Amish be able to continue their distinct way of life much as they have in the past?

Viewed from the outside, the Amish are an anachronism, a people misplaced in time, or an ethnic community that will eventually be assimilated into the mainstream of American life. Although sociologists point to effective techniques of isolation, such as a distinctive dress, language, and rural life, these alone cannot explain Amish survival.

The Amish themselves are keenly aware of their strengths and weaknesses. Although they are strongly attached to the past, they live in the present. Their past is alive in their present. They accept the biblical teaching of the end of the world followed by a final judg-

Hard work, love of the land, and a contented life lie ahead.

Photo by Charles S. Rice

ment, but they are not preoccupied with waiting for the return of Christ. Nor do they speculate about the nature of life after death. The best preparation for the future, in their view, is faithfulness to the believing community which they express by going about their daily work and duties. The Amish assert that "no one knows the time of Christ's coming" but that a person must be ready, for "the one shall be taken, and the other left" (Matthew 24:40).

When the nuclear reactor accident occurred at Three Mile Island in Pennsylvania in 1979, most Amish were unaware of the event or the danger until they were approached by reporters a week later. Similarly, when the end of the world comes, the Amish hope to be found doing their normal duties faithfully.

The Amish know that the maintenance of a redemptive community is a delicate function. The priorities of such a church-community are unity, sacrificial suffering, brotherly love, humility, and peaceableness. As a corporate offering to God, such a community must constantly strive to be worthy as "a bride for the groom."

"My life is happy," said one Amishman. "We are no less happy than people of any other religion. We plan for the future. We live on hopes and hard work. And we enjoy our life more than people who feel free to have anything in the world they please."

Perhaps the modern hurried, worried world could learn something from the Amish.

Selected Readings

Amish Cooking. Published by Herald Press, Scottdale, Pa., and Personal Library Publishers, Toronto, 1980. 318 pp.

Budget, The. Sugarcreek, Ohio 44681. A weekly newspaper serving the Amish and Mennonite communities.

Fisher, Gideon L. *Farm Life and Its Changes*. Gordonville, Pa.: Pequea Publishers, 3981 E. Newport Road, 1978. 384 pp. An Amish farmer describes Lancaster County agriculture.

Hostetler, John A. *Amish Society*. Baltimore, Md.: Johns Hopkins University Press, 1980. 416 pp. General description of history and culture.

Hostetler, John A. and Huntingdon, Gertrude E. *Children in Amish Society*. New York: Holt, Rinehart, Winston, 1971. 120 pp. Discusses Amish education in detail.

Keim, Albert. *Compulsory Education and the Amish*. Boston: Beacon Press, 1975. 212 pp. Discusses the Amish struggle for religious liberty.

Klees, Frederic. *The Pennsylvania Dutch*. New York: Macmillan, 1950. 452 pp. Excellent description of all Pennsylvania German groups, with a chapter on the Amish.

Pathway Publishing Corporation, Lagrange, Ind. 46761, and Route 4, Aylmer, Ontario N5H 2R3. Publishers of Amish periodicals and books.

Schreiber, William I. *Our Amish Neighbors*. Chicago, Ill.: University of Chicago Press, 1962. 228 pp. Discusses the Ohio Amish.

Schweider, Elmer and Dorothy. *A Peculiar People: Iowa's Old Order Amish*. Ames, Iowa: Iowa State University Press, 1975. 188 pp.

Yoder, Joseph W. *Rosanna of the Amish*. Scottdale, Pa.: Herald Press. 315 pp. Describes the author's family; fictional narrative and delightful.